LOST IN CASE

CAREN FLORANCE

Other publications by Caren Florance

POETRY

The Future, Unimagine (with Angela Gardner)
Members Only (with Melinda Smith)
Proseity
Tracer (with Owen Bullock)

SELECTED ARTIST BOOKS

1962: Be Spoken To (with Melinda Smith)
Elegy to Lost Times
Interference (with Angela Gardner)
Pleasure Demolition (with Angela Gardner)
Pr0n Coktales
Tag Urself: I'm the spiky one
Those Who Travel (with Sarah Rice & Patsy Payne)
Tracer: You Are Here (with Owen Bullock & Louise Curham)
Working Papers: hone/torrent (with Angela Gardner)
WYSIWYG

LOST IN CASE

CAREN
FLORANCE

CorditeBooks

First printed in 2019
by Cordite Publishing Inc.

PO Box 393
Carlton South 3053
Victoria, Australia
cordite.org.au | korditebooks.org.au

National Library of Australia
Cataloguing-in-Publication:

Florance, Caren
Lost in Case
978-0-6485116-1-8 paperback
I. Title.
A821.3

Poetry set in Bembo 10 / 14
Cover design by Zoë Sadokierski
Text design by Kent MacCarter and Zoë Sadokierski
Printed and bound by McPherson's Printing, Maryborough, Victoria.

 Cordite Publishing Inc. thanks Caren Florance, Angela Gardner, Penelope Goodes and Bella Li for their input during the production and editing of this book.

10 9 8 7 6 5 4 3 2 1

For those that know the joy of inky fingers:
Primum non nocere

CONTENTS

PREFACE

Are you feeling helpless and angry? I am. I'm having a quiet rage against the material and immaterial machine. Thank you for holding me.

I really love using digital media, but I feel that we are close to the end of the beta phase of online freedom. At the start it was all memes and quizzes. Now we know that our inane quiz answers are being used against us in ways that we still haven't quite grasped. There is an undercurrent of darkness overflowing onscreen because thoughtless public articulation is at our fingertips, and much of it is aimed at women of all shapes, creeds and colours.

This book is a shard of frustration. It's a place to process emotion. Angry and curious, I recently dived into some dark online spaces that I hope one day will be lost, and documented words and phrases used about and against women. Many of them are ancient, others have a particularly digital twist. I've captured only a core sample. I wanted to process them with eye and hand, to visually transmit the grime and stab of these communications. I capture but simultaneously obfuscate, because too much of this culture relies on the thrill of being noticed.

Handset letterpress printing, the process that informs my broader creative practice, is slow and deliberate. You stand in front of a case (a type storage drawer), and each letter has to be picked up, moved and placed. Your whole arm is activated. There is time to think during the movements. It is profoundly different to typing. It's not better, just a different speed.

I'm working with the concept of printing itself: its terminology and actions are historically drawn from the human body. As an experimental letterpress printer, I often use words to give paper a hard time, and the audience can usually witness the marks left by my processes. In this physical book I have had to think flatter, within the restrictions of contemporary digital print processes. I've constructed the pages carefully to do a double play between two man-made print systems – analogue typesetting and digital keyboarding – that have at times actively discouraged the involvement of women in their activities. These are the kinds of things I think about as I work.

Lost in Case is closer to an artist book than a collection. It starts with letterpress word play, then shifts to letterpress movements: gestural, abstracted translations of words and phrases used in contemporary online attacks on women, communications that seem immaterial and fleeting on page and screen but sink deep into the psyche. They are sharp, pointy, energetic pulses. They are able to be decoded, depending on what a fellow artist calls your 'curiosity threshold'. Transmitting these words without reseeding their message is a cathartic act of feminist disruption. The results seem impenetrable, but they can, with careful attention, be restored if desired. Or not: some things might be better lost.

INTRODUCTION

Caren Florance works in the Venn overlaps of text art, visual poetry and creative publishing. Her work is hard to pin down, principally because the artist herself is not interested in a static outcome. Much of the work appears as a flux, a process or a continuum along a moving line that often explores language and our usage of it.

Take letterpress – the method of using moveable type to print multiple copies. In some of Florance's work, the letterpress is not even printed as words (the expected or usual outcome of ink on paper, or at least ink on printable surface). Instead, what you see is the process of arriving (or not arriving) at the print. The California job case holds individual pieces of moveable type: there is one rectangular box for each letter, each space, each mark of punctuation. As the hand reaches across the case to pick each piece from its box, lines of movement are created. These lines are recorded by Florance with drawn lines: in this book, words are substituted for diagrams of movement.

As readers of these visual poems we are slowed down so that the meaning embodied in the method itself is made visible. A space in this system, for instance, has weight and heft, it is a metal piece that has its own positive presence in the type case. You reach for it as you would the space bar on a Qwerty typewriter and it yields the same result: a nothing that is a something, between other somethings. The typist knows the work of reaching for and touching that space; the reader, in the rush to get to the meaning, may forget.

Language is performative, and the words Florance has chosen to work with in *Lost in Case* have particular meanings and histories. Many are drawn from vocabularies of abuse, or shaming, of female bodies, or commentary on the availability of those bodies for the sexual use of men. The language is brutal and is taken from spaces that have not been friendly towards women: from misogynist male-only forums to incel chat rooms, for self-identified and angry involuntary celibates. With autonomous AI-informed sex-bots on the horizon, issues of determination and consent will continue to be foregrounded. Will a compliant human-like sex toy serve to reinforce the mistaken entitlement of the incels?

Using these words here is not self-abuse. Instead, Florance counters sloppy online reasoning, which seems to elide issues of self-determination and consent, with a rigorous analogue Teknik. She takes control of the gestures behind the words, to render the abuse as visual poetry. Florance's aim to transmit the words again without reseeding their message is, in her words, 'a cathartic act of feminist disruption'. Working from a theory of forensic materiality – informed by the work of academics Matthew Kirschenbaum, Jerome McGann and N Katherine Hayles – Florance makes something that seems impenetrable and lost to meaning able to be translated by forensic means. The word 'forensic' reminds us that words have heft, they take shape. How should we react to these words? Instead of allowing misogynistic language to proliferate in the self-reinforcing echo chambers of online forums, we must take it out into the light and examine what animates it. For some women this will become a matter of life or death.

—Angela Gardner

SET

[redacted] [redacted]

[redacted] [redacted] [redacted] [redacted] [redacted] [redacted] [redacted] [redacted]

[redacted] [redacted] [redacted] [redacted] [redacted] [redacted] [redacted] [redacted]

[redacted] [redacted]
[redacted] [redacted] [redacted] [redacted] [redacted]
[redacted]

k j

g f s i e d c b

w q y o h n m l

p z

r a t u v

x

YOU TURN

(WHAT IS) SWAPPED (IS) SWAPPED (AND)
WON'T COME BACK

B
Y
T
T

NEVER FULLY REDACTED

LEAD WEIGHT

T [redacted] A T
D U M [redacted]
S [redacted] U T
C [redacted] N T
S L [redacted] G
M [redacted] L L

EYE SORE

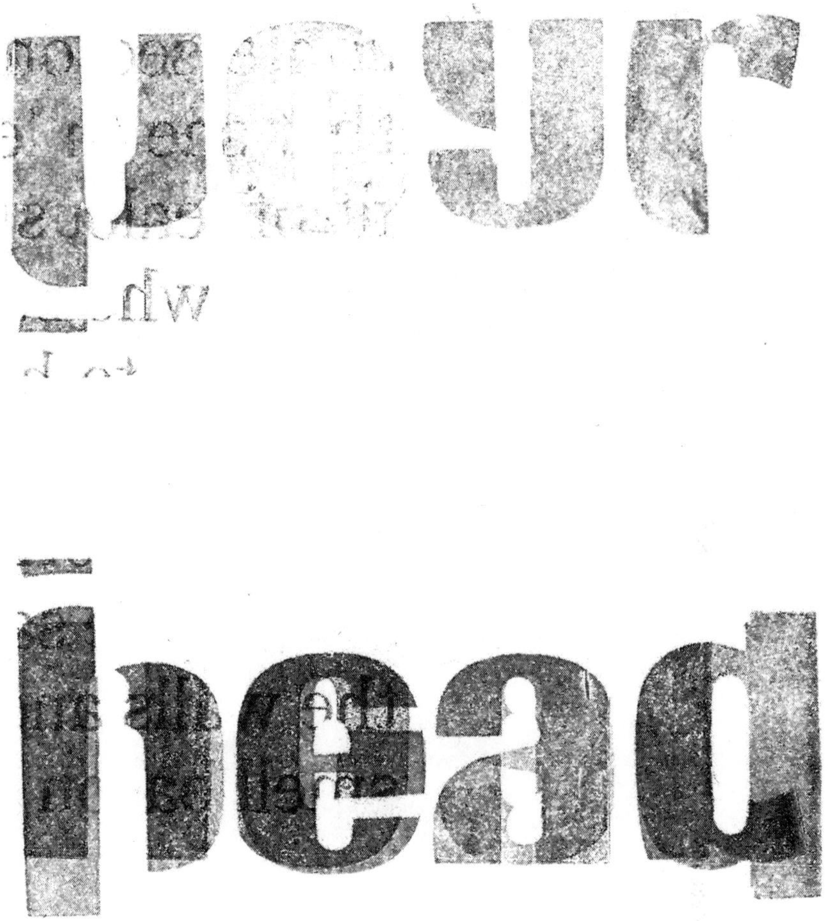

_ O W _ _ S

[redacted]a[redacted]

[redacted]e

[redacted]i[redacted]

[redacted]o[redacted]

u[redacted]

FINGERED

LETTER ESS

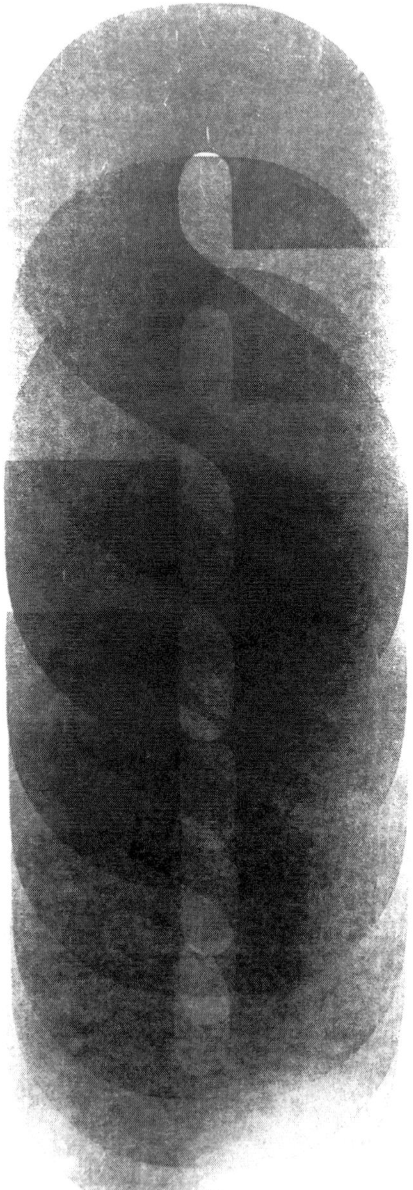

CHOOSE A FACE YOU CAN LIVE WITH

If you choose an odd sort of face you will find its peculiarities, which may have been attractive at first sight, become more of an eyesore as you grow familiar with them and compare them with the astonishing beauty of normal

HONE

hardly moves tiy truck broken glass and rotten goop
reclusive hollow and high note a large dog anp a small
dog in the process oJ its own making had we stayed the
fallout colla,sing time contingent s ill the morning the
bone water of self Sone sasling this is not preɪty ,oetry displac
gone

contingents ill
contingent s will
s till
s hill
s pill
s kill

[redacted]

[redacted] [redacted] [redacted] [redacted]

moist mess
mass
miss
mrs
mss
manuscript indent note
rote

right error possibic contingent up on geeling awkward

bright error

feeling awkward
peeling
reeling
geiling
gentling
greeding

pol[redacted]tesse each listening elsewhere where as we listen again
fresn dtive moist mrss indent note tri stave coast scurvy lug
inch idea tighy rapid joy se[redacted] in sunglasses slight working
late night music actuallo soneone dlse all direction[redacted]

drive
active
additive
dice
directive

set
sec
sea
sew
sell
sex in sunglasses
unglasses
lasses

head

untouched edges

body

double

gathering

gutter

DUMMY

opening

spread

signatures

tail

PARTS

face
beard
counter
shoulder
height
set/width
groove
nick
feet

CHASE (HOLDING FRAME)

A B C D E F G

H I K L M N O

P Q R S T V W

X Y Z U J

A FIRST BLAST OF THE TRUMPET AGAINST THE MONSTROUS

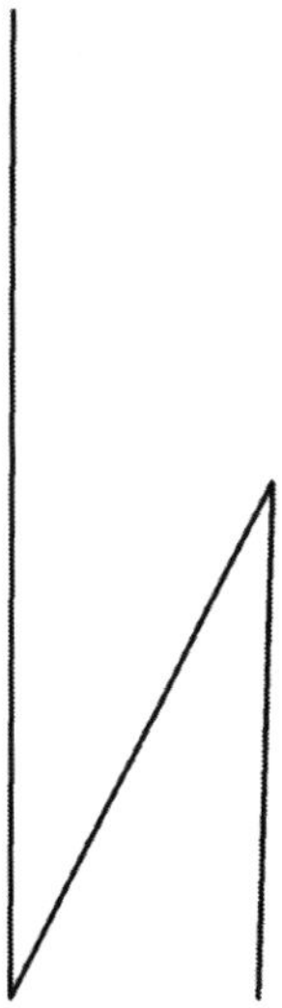

BOYS WILL BE BOYS

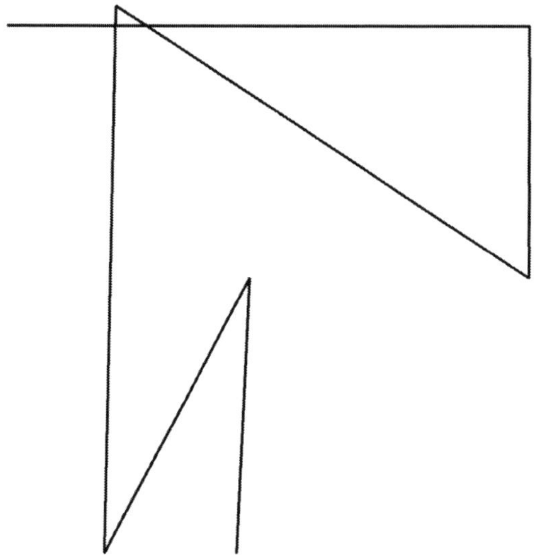

CONTROLLING YOUR FEAR WITH FAITH

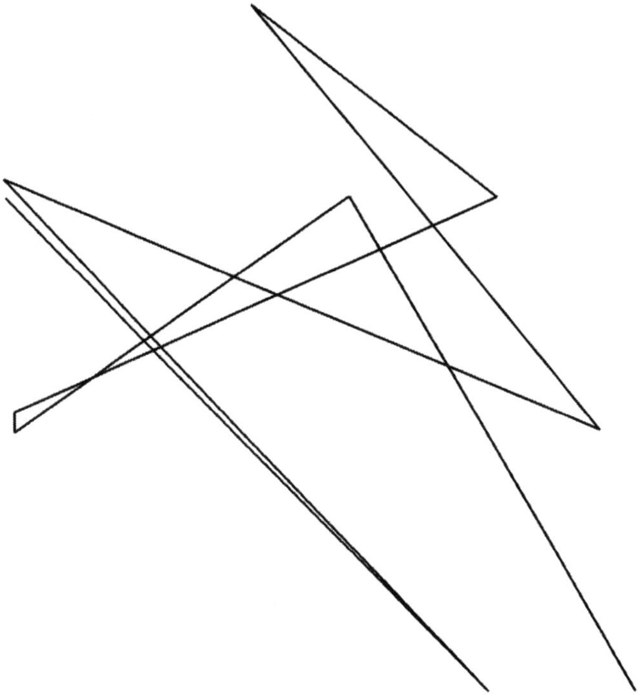

DON'T RAIN ON MY PARADE

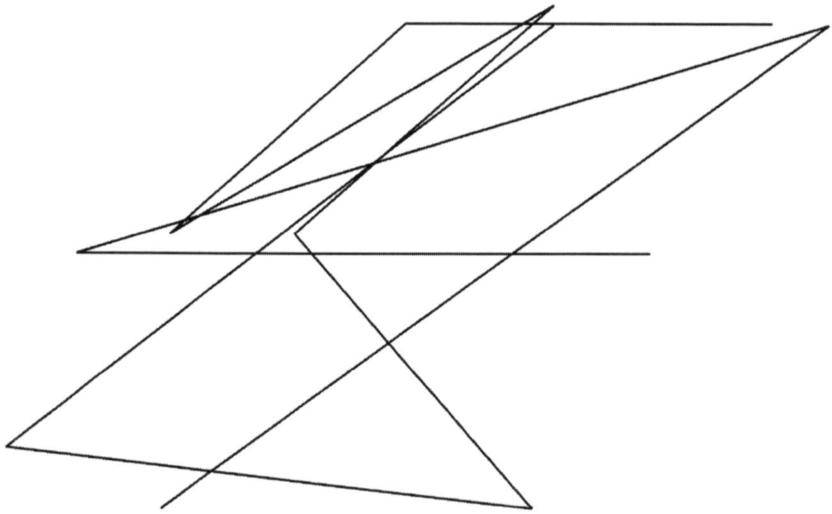

EVERY GOOD BOY DESERVES F*

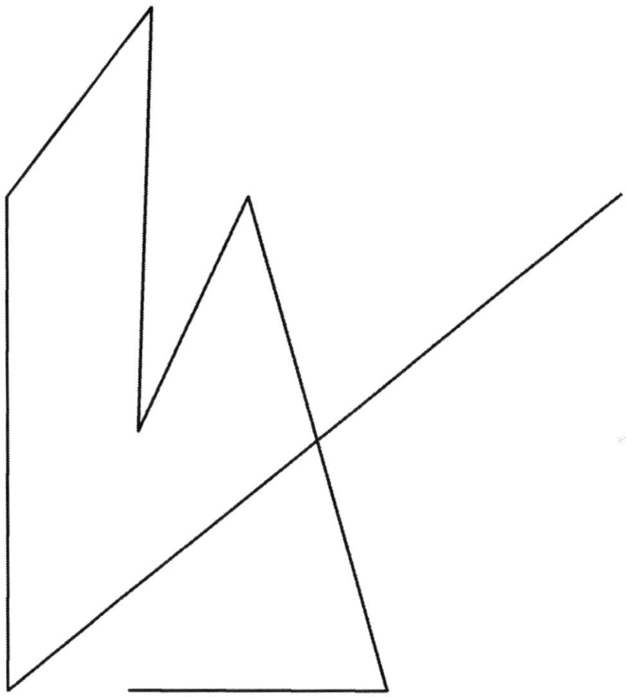

FIRST PRINCIPLES THINKING

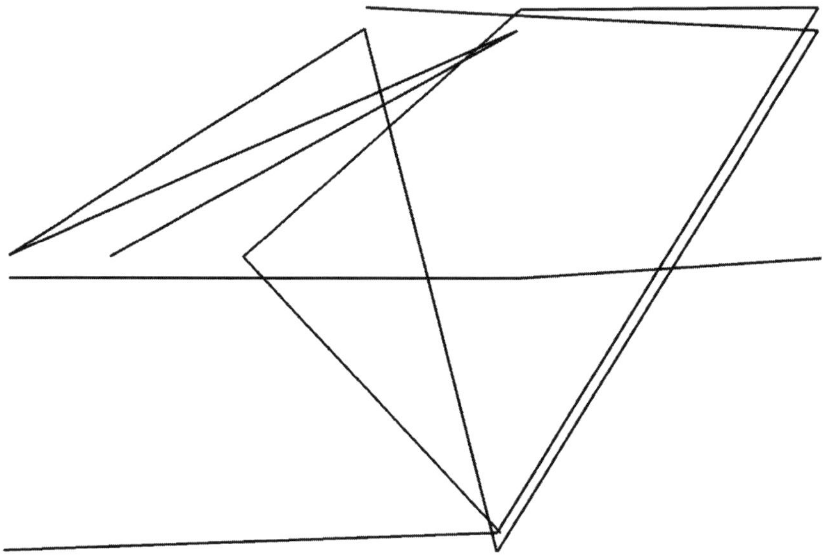

GOOD BOYS DO FINE

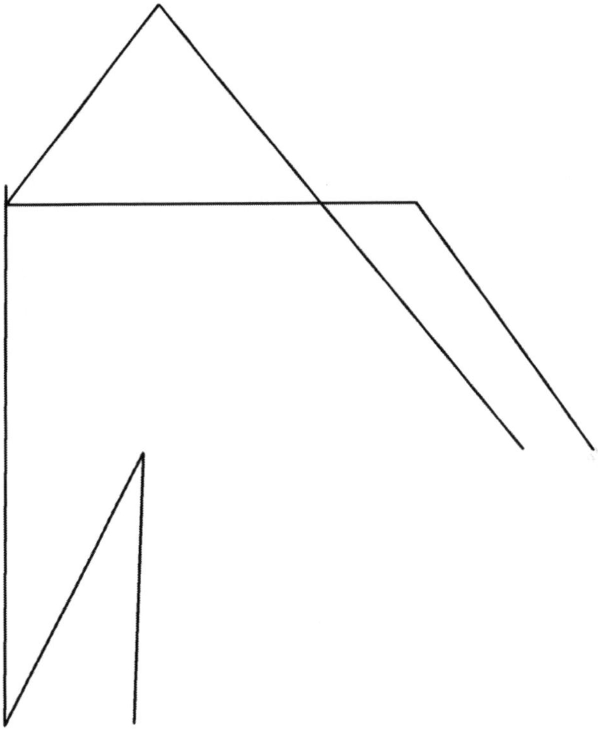

HYPERGAMY

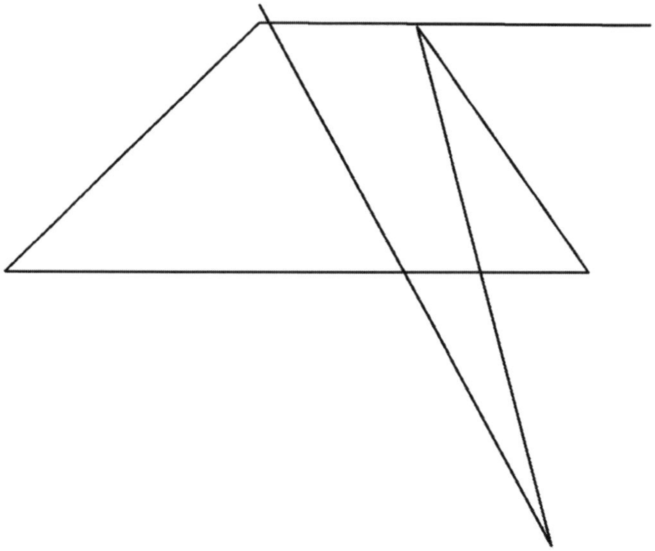

INCELSPHERE

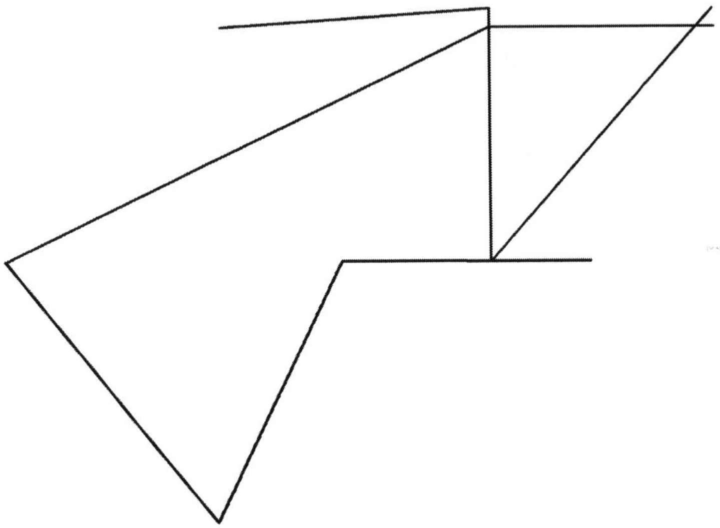

KITTENFISHING

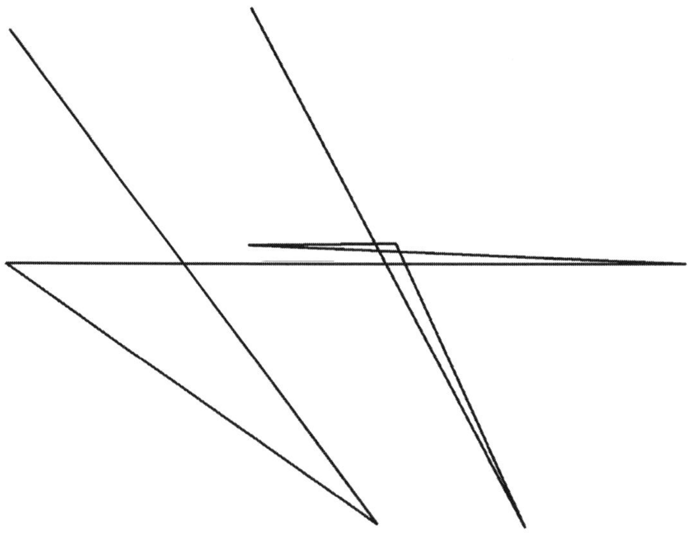

LITERALLY WHO

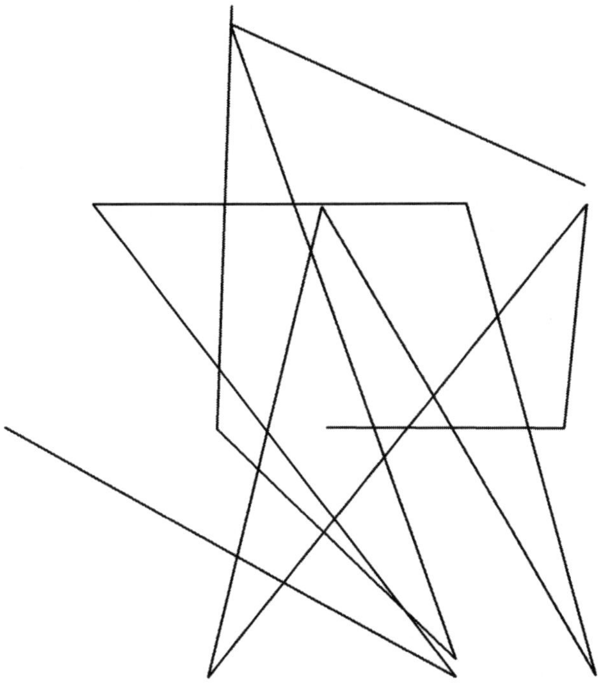

MANBABY

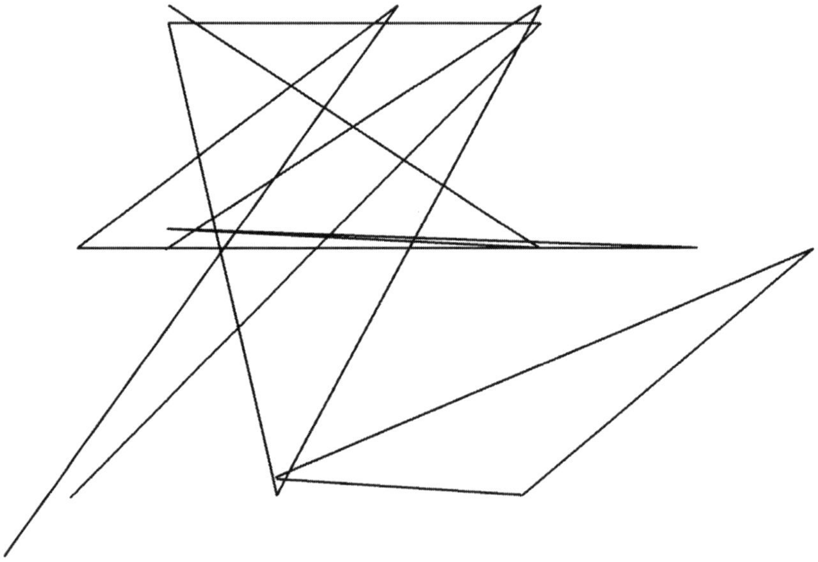

NEGOTIABLE ASSETS

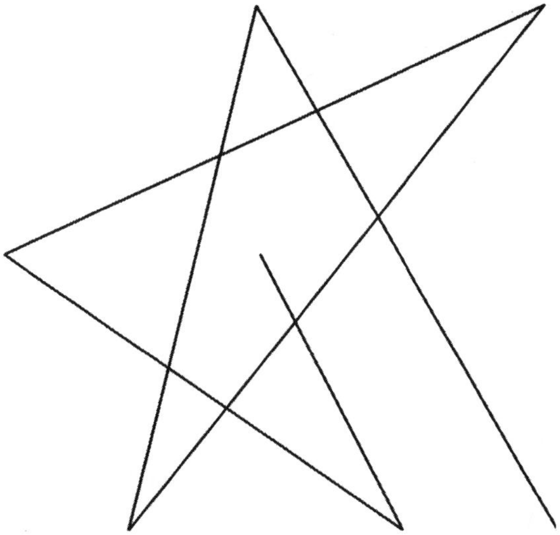

OPPOSITION LEADER

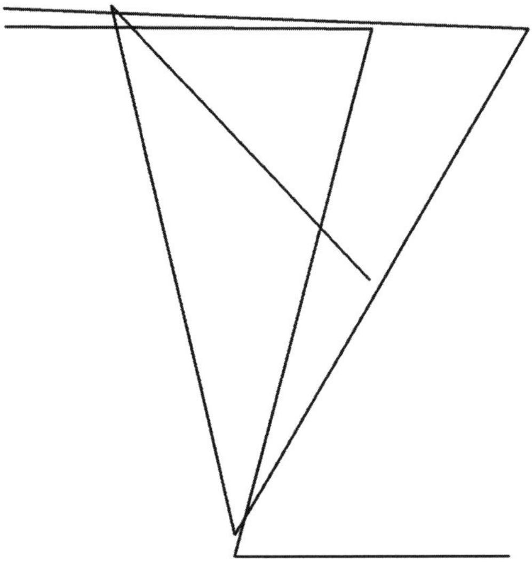

PISR R

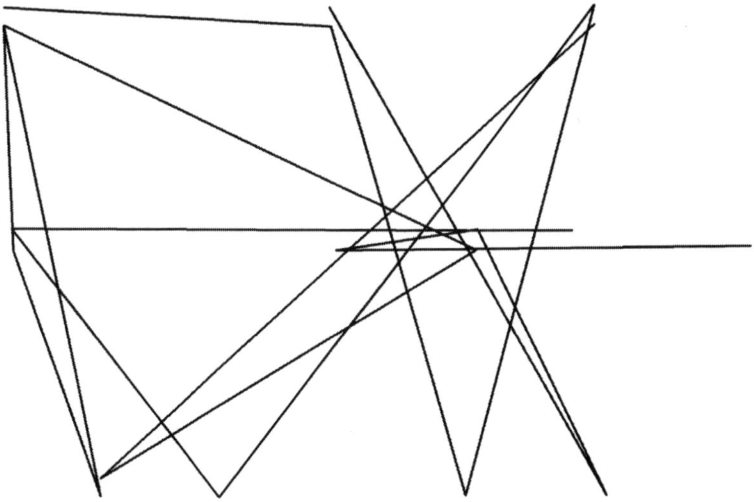

QUALIFIED ADMIRATION

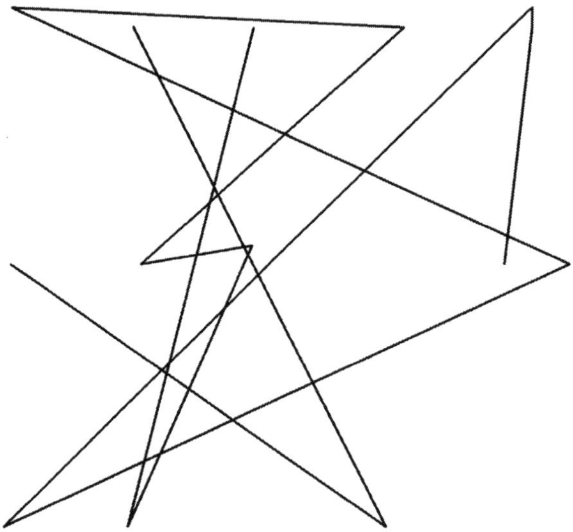

RULE 34

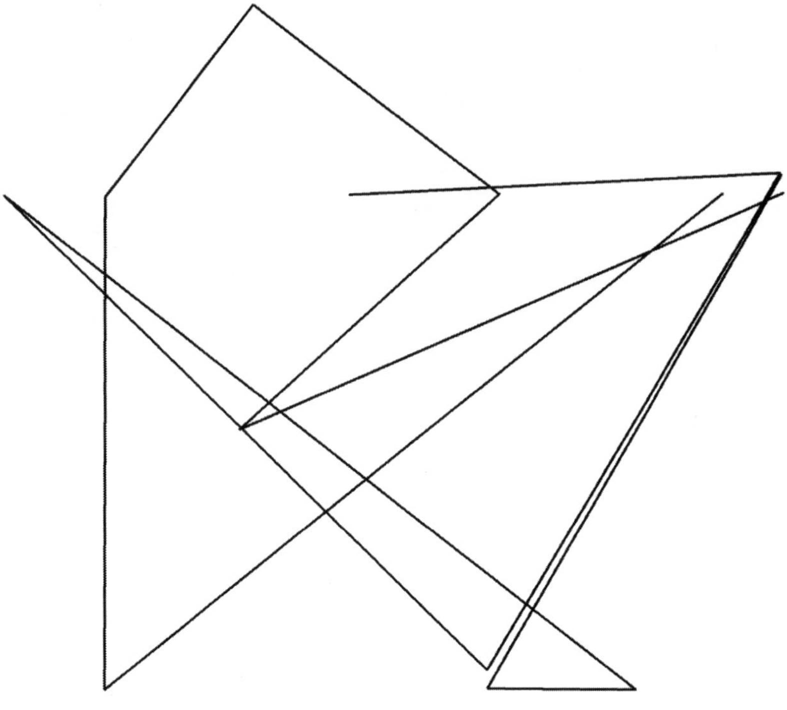

SPLIT MATING MARKET

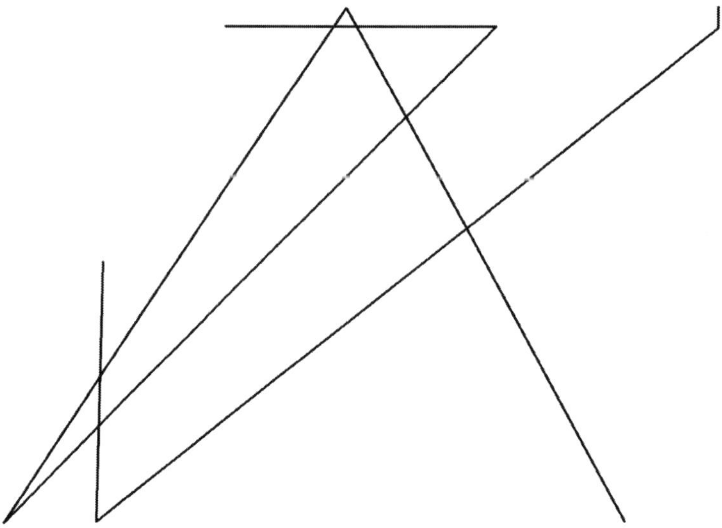

TROLL PRIDE WORLDWIDE

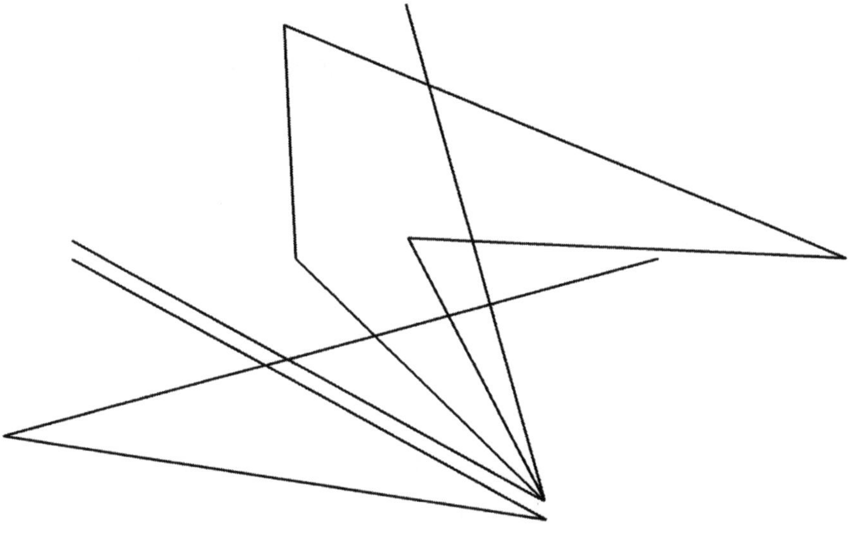

VIKINGS DO THEY STILL EXIST

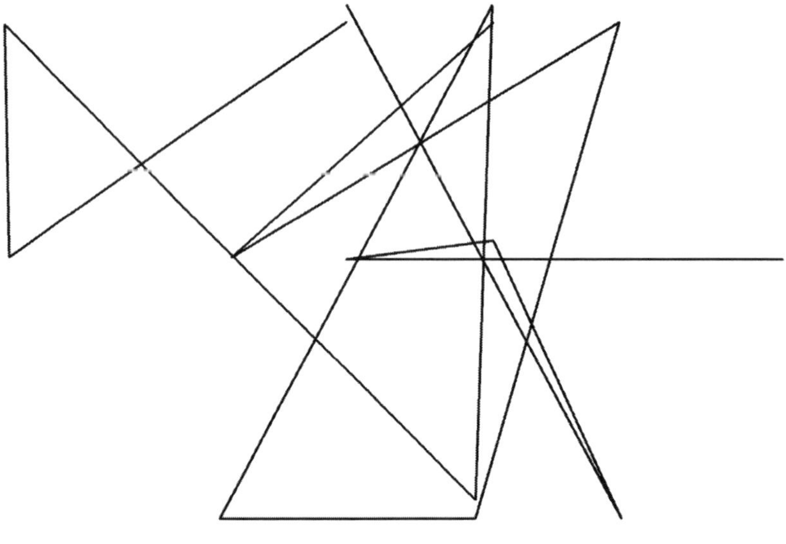

WEEKEND HOBBIES

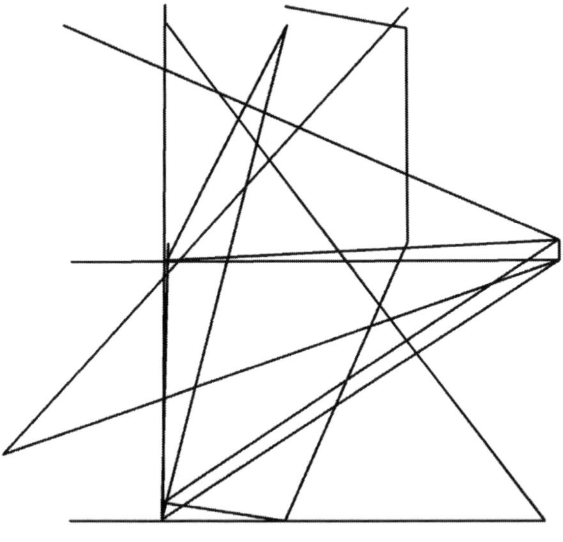

XBOX CONTROLLER

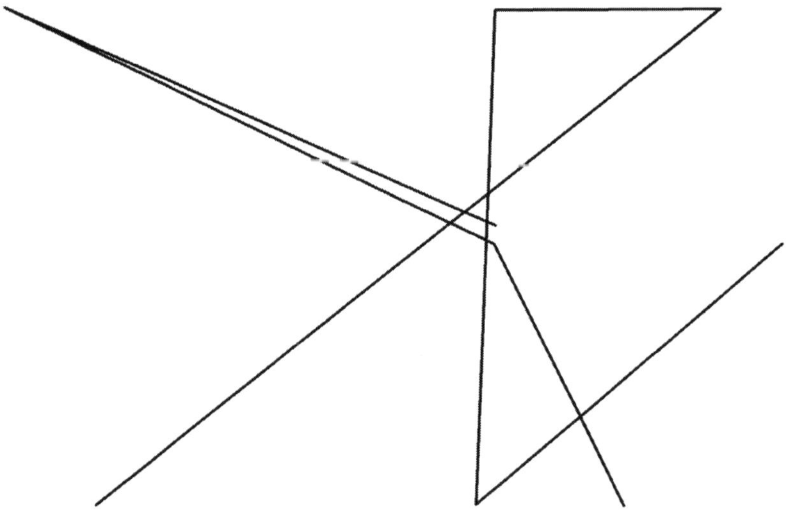

YOUR MOM

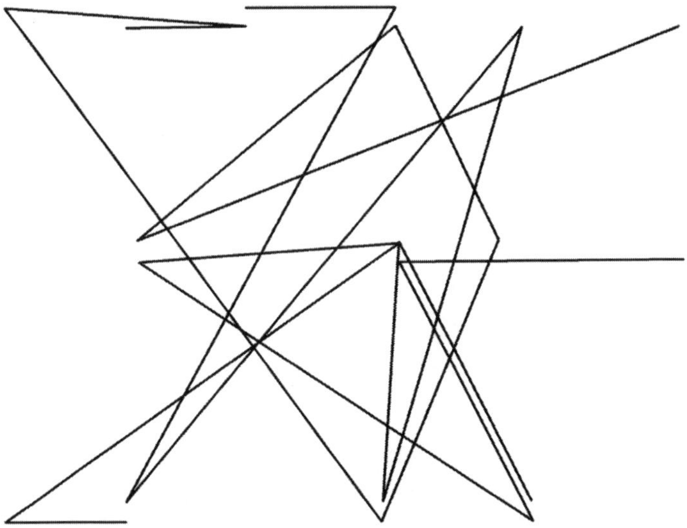

ZEUS IS AN EXAMPLE OF A TROJAN HORSE

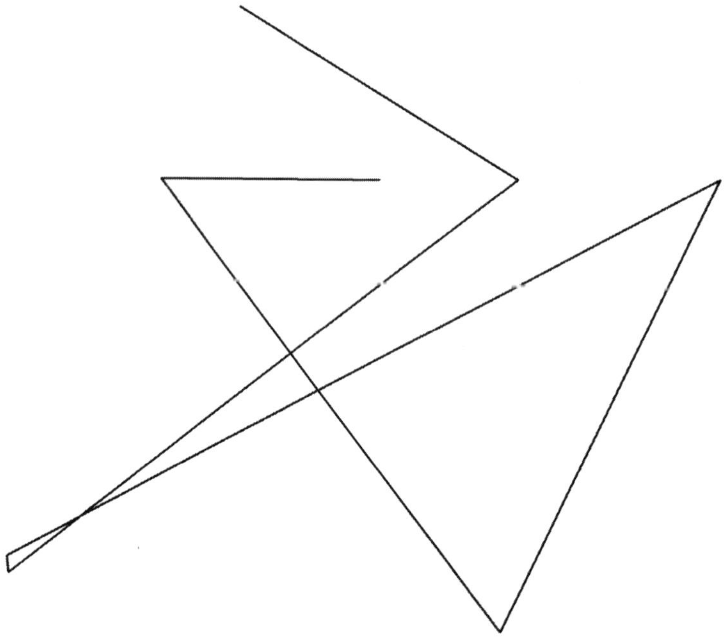

JOKE, JOYCE

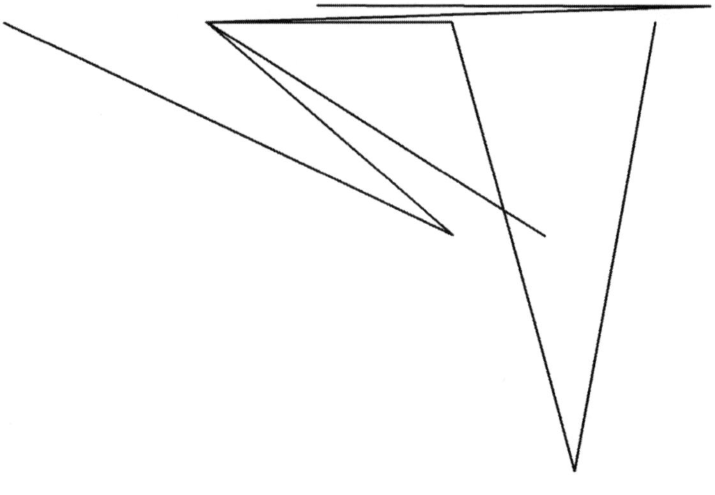

UNILATERAL ACTION

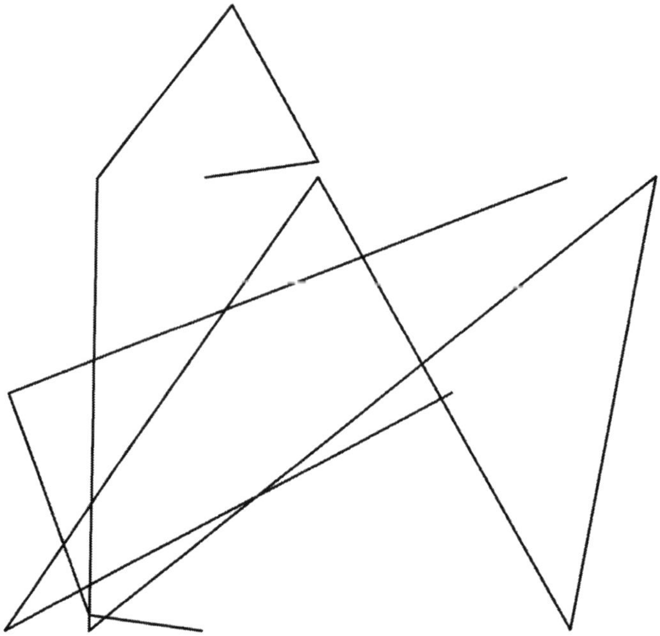

DIY

: :

: : : : : : : :

: : : : : : : :

: :

: : : : :

:

DIS

[redacted] [redacted] [redacted] [redacted] [redacted] [redacted] [redacted] [redacted] [redacted] [redacted]
[redacted] [redacted] [redacted] [redacted] [redacted] [redacted] [redacted] [redacted] [redacted]
[redacted] [redacted] [redacted] [redacted] [redacted] [redacted] [redacted]

DIS

tribute

sent

respect

assemble

miss

TROUBLE & STRIFE

PLAYING THE GENDER CARD

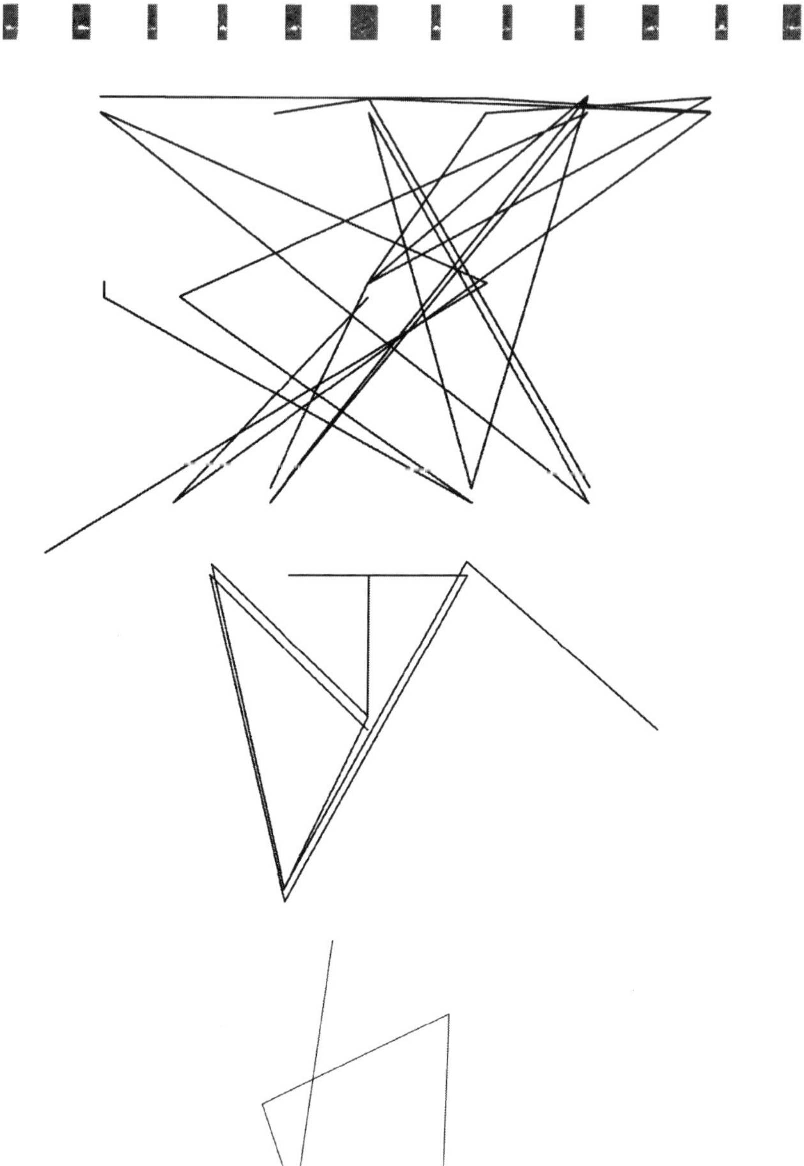

OH MY DARLING

BEAR HUG

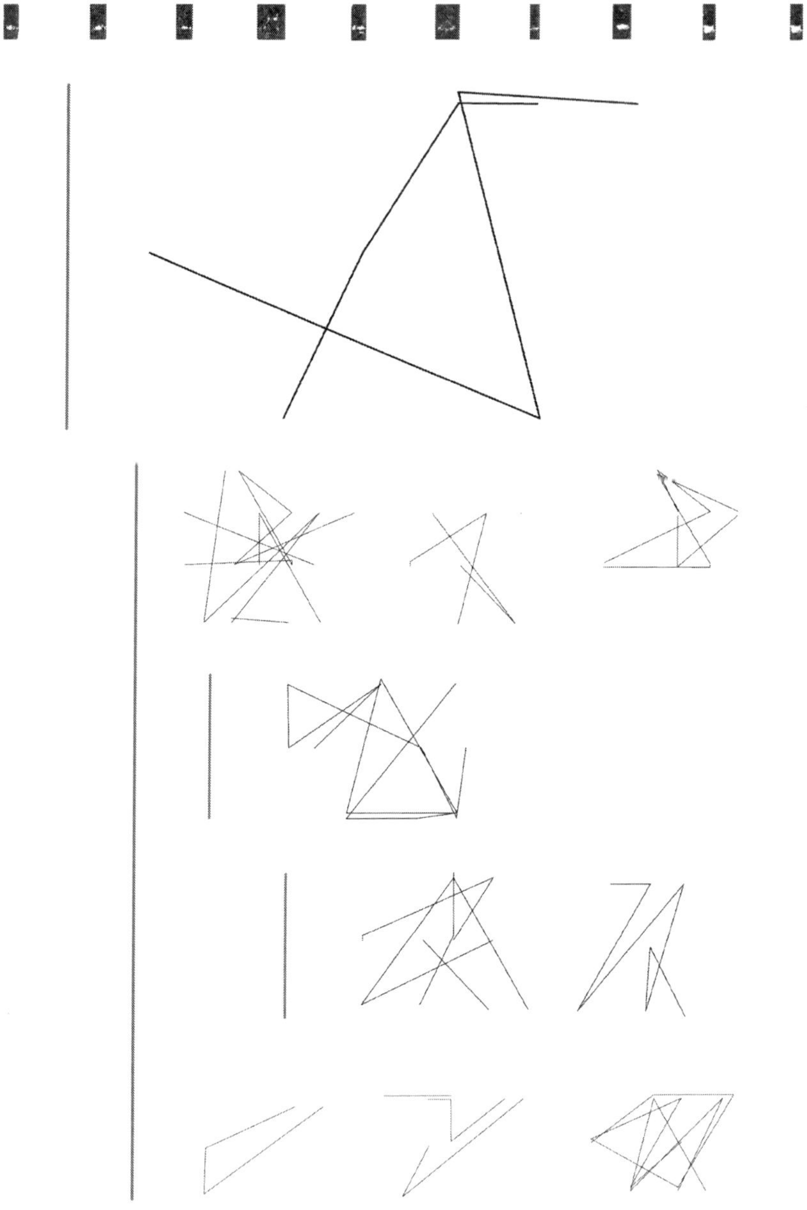

POOR IMPULSE CONTROL

SUGGESTIONS WELCOME

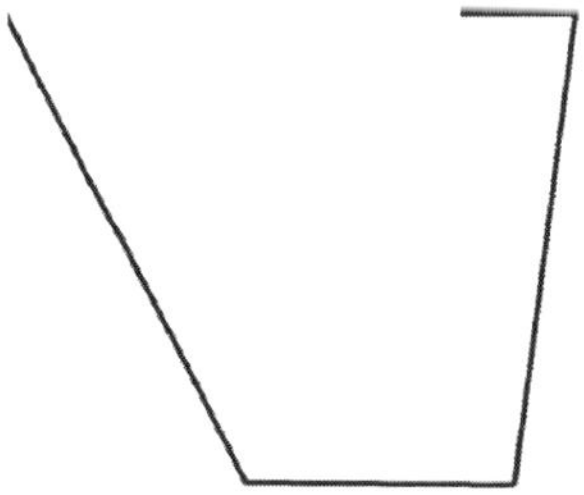

NOTES

The type-case layout I'm using, the California job case (CJC), is to many printers what the qwerty keyboard is to computers. It has its idiosyncrasies, particularly in the placement of the uppercase *J* and *U*, which were separated from the rest of the alphabet because they didn't exist in Latin, a language whose dominance ended well before California was invented. (This says a lot about man-made systems.) The CJC also has regional variations: in Australia, the lowercase *j* is in a different place to the New Zealand case layout, and both are different to the layout of the Northern Hemisphere. Sometimes the lowercase *x* and *z* are transposed as well. Don't even get me started on where the punctuation and numbers usually go, so they've been omitted here.

Pages 5-7: These letterpress prints are vintage woodtype on 140gsm Madrid Litho paper, 700 x 450mm. Printed at the Centre for Print Research, University of West England Ashton Bower Campus, September 2018. Exhibited in *We are Lost* at Megalo Print Studios + Gallery, Canberra, October 2018.

Page 8: 'Lead Weight', printed for *Axon Analogue* 6, a staff letterpress folio printed by members of the Centre for Creative and Cultural Research, University of Canberra, 2018.

Page 9: 'Eye Sore', letterpress overprint, studio experimentation, 2014.

Page 11: 'Fingered', original letterpress monotype on 300gsm Fabriano Rosapina paper, printed in the Ampersand Duck studio, 2011. Private collection.

Page 12: 'Letter Ess', original print titled *Ess 9*, woodtype printed with graphite ink on Kozo Light washi, 710 x 510mm. Printed in the ANU Printmedia & Drawing Book Workshop, Canberra. Thanks to John Pratt for finding the large *S* block, forever separated from its fellow letters. Exhibited in Letter Ess at Canberra Contemporary Art Space, Canberra, January 2016.

Page 13: Quote from p 44 of John Ryder's *Printing for Pleasure* (London: English Universities Press, 1957).

Page 14: 'Hone' letterpress excerpts from Angela Gardner & Caren Florance, *Working Papers: hone/torrent*, 2014-17. Artist books, letterpress on Gyokurya washi, variable edition of 3.

Pages 23–51: 'Chase (Holding Frame)' is a unique artist book consisting of carbon drawings and typewritten text on white index cards, housed in a black card case. First shown in *Line Work*, Tuggeranong Arts Centre, 4–27 July, 2019. There is a companion set consisting of red carbon drawings on black card, called *Blind Rage*. They don't want to be translated into black and white.

Pages 61–67: 'Poor Impulse Control' is also an artist book consisting of red pencil hand-coloured onto laserprinted pages, concertinaed into a black Stonehenge 245gsm paper cover. Edition of 6. First shown in *Line Work*, Tuggeranong Arts Centre, 4–27 July, 2019.

Everything else is easily Googled.*

*If Google / Reddit / the internet does not exist when you are reading this, how excellent!

ACKNOWLEDGEMENTS

A huge thank you to Kent MacCarter for making this book happen.

Thank you to Angela Gardner for her generous introduction, and to Bella Li and Zoë Sadokierski.

I am profoundly grateful to everyone at the University of Canberra's Centre for Creative and Cultural Research; they are a generous and supportive community. Much of this work was done during my time as the CCCR 2018 Donald Horne Creative and Cultural Fellow.

Gratitude also to Sarah Bodman and Angela Butler at the Centre for Fine Print Research of the University of West England Bower Ashton Campus for their hard work around the book as art, and for a fabulous week of printing and conversing in September 2018.

Thank you to Megalo Print Studio + Gallery and Tuggeranong Arts Centre for exhibiting many of these works.

Thanks also to the staff of the ANU Printmedia & Drawing Workshop for their support, institutional and otherwise.

Love and thanks to all my friends and family, past and present.

Caren Florance was born in Wagga Wagga in 1967. After a childhood of moving around with her military family, she settled in Canberra to attend the ANU (because university was free then). She studied classics, English literature and women's studies. After that she went to university again, at UNSW Canberra (because it was fun) and did a Pass Masters in English literature. There she stumbled across the letterpress process during a bibliography course. She then went to the ANU School of Art (because it had letterpress equipment), and she's been there ever since. She teaches as a sessional lecturer, and makes artwork and printed matter, sometimes under the imprint Ampersand Duck.

She recently completed a PhD in creative practice at the University of Canberra, where she now teaches within its Visual Communications degree. She has produced numerous artist books, both solo and collaboratively. Her work is collected nationally and internationally, mostly by libraries. She has written reviews and articles for publications such as *Art Monthly*, *Artlink*, *Cordite Poetry Review*, *foam-e*, *Imprint* and *Script & Print*.